Contents

~CHAPTER 1~

The Power of Knowledge

Destruction of conditioning

~CHAPTER 2~

The Evolution of Consciousness

Invention of Writing

~CHAPTER 3~

The Destruction of Knowledge

Era of Dangerous Books

~CHAPTER 4~

Human's Center of Perception

The Brain

~CHAPTER 5~

The Teaching of Symmetry

Ancestral Wisdom

~CHAPTER 6~

The Law of Universal Balance

Conservation of Energy

~CHAPTER 7~

The Story of a Human Bat

Mental Reconfiguration

~CHAPTER 8~

The Ultimate Consciousness

Higher Level of Being

~CHAPTER 9~

The Effects of Memory

Amnesic Induction

~CHAPTER 10~

Ancient Secrets

Zombification

~CHAPTER 11~

Extra

Relativity of God

Acknowledgements

I dedicated this volume of ***The Last Stratum*** to my Mom and Dad. They could not understand what I was writing about. However, they have recognized that I was writing for an excellent cause. As my Dad always says, "Continue doing what you are doing."

I owe thanks to every member of my family for allowing me to spend years in isolation studying for tests, researching and writing this volume.

I owe gratitude to my brothers for their supports and recommendations. They could not wait to see this book published. They are aware of the objective and the motivation that drive me.

I owe many thanks to my uncle, Mr. Levit, for his continuing support in translating this book into French.

I do not know how many thanks to give to my dear friend and partner, Katehis Bartholomew, for designing the cover of this book, to help it out on time.

Guirand Michel

The Last Stratum
By
Guirand Michel

"You will know the truth, and the truth will set you free." _Jesus Christ, the Bible, John 8:32

~CHAPTER 1~

The Power of Knowledge
Destruction of conditioning

KNOWLEDGE-- like any dangerous weapon, to be effective, the physical and spiritual strength of the person in charge of it must be conditioned. However, the invention of writing has violated this condition.

The invention of writing is one of the greatest inventions of humankind. Amazingly, writing has elevated human's intellect to a higher degree. It allows the spreading of advanced information to circulate accurately from one generation to the next. In fact, before the development of writing, advanced information used to be passed on from one individual to another by word of mouth. During that era, the process of information transfer was not only tedious but also difficult.

Moreover, it required certain individuals to be carefully selected to acquire advanced knowledge. In many instances, people responsible for receiving advanced information must be put to the test. Usually, an assessment of physical and mental strength was necessary before an individual could have access to certain types of knowledge. Among certain esoteric sects, this procedure was excellent and deserved considerable importance, for it prevents certain individuals from misusing advanced information. Often, members of certain cults, magical societies, African tribes and esoteric sects believe some people possess the negative tendency to exploit and abuse superior knowledge. Therefore, they could cause pain, suffering and misery to innocent beings. In that sense, it is noble to keep divine knowledge off these hands. However, such severe measure about advanced knowledge has its disadvantages.

As time passes, human's memory becomes fragile and weak. Hence, incredible, advanced knowledge tends to fade away and degenerate into the past. During old age, memory is beginning to become extremely difficult to access. Unfortunately, ordinary consciousness rearranges memory in a linear fashion (The Last Stratum, Volume II). In ordinary consciousness, human memory is not suitable to store non-survival events for a long time. Within certain African tribes, spiritual techniques such as the practices of burning specific herbs have been developed to assist the keepers of knowledge. It was common that especial magical portions could help one to access old memories of his ancestors. However, the passing of an individual elder that carries a vast amount of divine knowledge could be devastated to the knowledge bank of a tribe. Such credence was accepted because certain information was regarded as extremely perilous.

In reality, there is nothing dangerous in having knowledge. In fact, having knowledge could be one of the greatest things in the world. What we should remember is: The human psyche in possession of advanced information could be more dangerous than the knowledge it contains. Hence, an immature human mind could be more dangerous than anything else. It is the most dangerous thing ever. Therefore, to protect and defend the human race, advanced knowledge is declared sacred.

~CHAPTER 2~

The Evolution of Consciousness

Invention of Writing

WRITING revolutionized the human mind. It motivates the intellectuals to write inspiring manuscripts to immortalize their discoveries, their souls, their era and their awareness. Before the invention of the printing press, in Europe and around the world, it was difficult for the average person to have access to advanced information. Books were not only incredibly expensive they were also regulated. Furthermore, established inquisitions of the Catholic Church had control over every form of written information. Moreover, one could not write anything hat disagreed with the view of the Catholic Church. Anyone who violated this condition risked facing death at the stake.

Apparently, certain religious practices were typically designed to nurture ignorance and exploit the people. Because it is difficult to abuse and exploit intelligent human beings, man must be kept under delusion and ignorance for certain religions to succeed. A ridiculous practice of ancient priests of the Catholic Church was to allow people to pay for their sins, using indulgences. Therefore, only the wealthy can go to heaven.

Indulgences could not be printed fast enough because of the limitation in printing technology. In Germany, at around the 1940's, the church hired Johannes Gutenberg to print indulgences. Gutenberg was frustrated. He could not make enough money because he was unable to print indulgences fast enough. The contemporary system of printing was too slow. Gutenberg inspired to invent a device capable of printing indulgences faster. He invented a more advanced printing press, way better than the previous ones. This incredible invention revolutionized the world of printing. It allowed the transfer of information to be much faster than before. Gutenberg started by printing many bibles for the church. At that time, a priest was the only person permitted to own a copy of the Bible. During this era, the Bible was printed in nonliving languages such as Greek and Latin; it was not authorized to translate into any other languages. The church utilized various tricks with the objective to oppress the people and force them to accept its doctrine without questions. Only a few scholars were able to understand Latin. Among them, William Tyndale of England took the liberty to translate the Bible into German. This mistake eventually cost him his life. He was found guilty and burnt alive at the stake.

Gutenberg's invention allowed the production of books to be not only easy but also affordable. Books started to be everywhere. Anyone was able to obtain fascinating manuscripts containing advanced information in the trash and at bargain prices. The people began to read the principles of the Bible, and the intelligent ones realized that the many so-called "high priests" were nothing but charlatans. As a result, they refused to pay for indulgences and soon revolted against the Catholic Church.

Gutenberg's printing press created the opportunity for the mass to accumulate advanced knowledge at an exponential rate. The accumulation of advanced knowledge has subtle effects on the human mind. It has the capability to improve the level of consciousness of the mass. Therefore, reduced the power of the church, where it could no longer control the distribution of information. Every day, hundreds of books were being printed. Stopping information from reaching the average person was no longer possible. Amazingly, anyone was able to buy a book to have access to whatever information he/she desires. Such incredible revolution upsets many elite societies. As a result, they have decided to prevent certain information from circulating through the public.

~CHAPTER 3~

The Destruction of Knowledge
Era of Dangerous Books

THROUGHOUT History, many books have been considered hazardous or evil. Some of these books have been denounced to contain critical information, and these books ended up being destroyed. To revolt against such dilemma, many authors were forced to write in code. The destruction process condemned many innocent writers whose intellect surpassed that of their contemporaries. Mistakes have been made. Many inexperienced writers have been killed. Hundreds of priceless manuscripts have been burned, and many authors have been banned from writing. Some books were considered highly dangerous; people argued that they caused harm to the reader's psyche. One of the first books in

History to be considered dangerous was that of **Thoth**.

Thoth was an Egyptian god with intelligence beyond normal human beings. He is associated with writing, mathematics, astrology and wisdom. It is said that Thoth was the inventor of writing and the logic of mathematics.

Thoth wrote a book, usually regarded to as ***The Book of Thoth,*** which contained incredible mathematical and astrological secrets that gave supernatural power to its readers. The book was presented in papyrus form. This book was burned, and during this period, King Ramesses III killed many who claimed to have read or used the book of Thoth. They were killed because news went out that many of these individuals formed an organized magical machination against the pharaoh. They secretly planned for the murder of the King during the Opet celebration. Unfortunately, their plan failed miserably. As a result, over fifty people were executed, and many committed suicide to avoid torture. People claimed that the book of Thoth armed the reader with the power to kill and curse his enemies at unlimited distances.

There is no doubt that the minds that can understand mathematics and astronomy are influential minds. Such minds deserve the greatest respect, for they are the key to the process of accelerated human development. On the contrary, the pharaoh's ignorance and insecurity led him to cruel atrocity against those advanced minds.

Another book that was classified as dangerous was written by a well-known American author, Lafayette Ron Hubbard. Hubbard was an officer in the Marines, a prolific writer and also a great explorer. During World War II, he was severely incapacitated and was hospitalized. During a near-death experience, Hubbard's eccentric mental state allowed him to access some of his inaccessible, primordial memory partitions. Amazingly, after he had finally brought back to normal living, he did not forget what he experienced. The memories he collected during a cataleptic state of mind remained with him.

Hubbard wrote a book entitled "Excalibur/ The Black Sword". Some individuals said that the book made people crazy. Some of his friends who read the book became aberrant individuals. Many religious people, as well as nonreligious people, were after the book. Their intention was not only to destroy the book but also to find out what kind of information was in it. Fortunately, Hubbard spent most of his life in a motorboat with the book locked securely in a drawer. The many attempts made to force the secured drawer were unsuccessful.

A lighter version of Hubbard's Excalibur appeared in another Hubbard's book titled "Dianetics". I read Dianetics many times because it is a good book (The Last stratum, Volume II); however, I can ensure you that I do not feel crazy. A friend of mine made an attempt to read Excalibur. He went to the Scientology office in Boston with the hope of securing a copy of Excalibur, and he was told by one of the auditors that this book does not exist anymore.

Those books that are considered dangerous are simply the clarification of an advanced expression of a human's degree of perception.

A long time ago, one of the books that claimed to contain the secrets of the earth and the sky was considered dangerous until it was found that this book only included a collection of first and second-degree mathematical equations. Of course, a book containing a collection of first and second-degree equations may not be the secret of the earth and the sky. However, a long time ago, before the mental re-evolution of man, such a book was obviously a step toward those secrets. The capability to solve first and second-degree mathematical equations gives mathematicians and scientists the mental power that helps them solve abstract mathematical and scientific problems.

Two questions arise: Is there such a thing as a dangerous book? How can a book be dangerous?

A book can be dangerous if it contains progressive ideas and falls into the hands of people whose psyches are poorly balanced. A book itself is not dangerous at all; the danger is in the reader's psyche. For instance, a pornographic magazine, a gun as well as a knife, in the hands of a five-year-old is automatically perceived as exceedingly dangerous. However, in the hands of a mentally stable, mature individual it is perfectly reasonable to a certain extent. The degree of danger of a book is in direct relation with the psyche of the reader. Such an argument reflects an example of the theory of relativity. *The Last Stratum* will prepare you to absorb and understand hidden aspects of the reality of the human spirit.

In Haiti, during the regime of Francois Duvalier, thousands of Haitian young men and women lost their lives. The Haitian people were denied the right to read any book containing Marxist ideologies. Any book written by the well-known German philosopher, Karl Marx, was considered dangerous. President Francois Duvalier passed the order to ban all books with Marxist ideologies and martial arts. Anyone found reading Marxist ideologies or practicing any form of martial arts would be put in jail for a long time or killed.

It exists countless legends and true stories about certain books that were not truly dangerous. In fact, the subject of dangerous books was raised as a prelude to introduce, *The Last Stratum*: A hot soup for the body and the soul of humanity.

During the era of dangerous books, *The Last Stratum* could have been classified as one of the dangerous books. It does not contain the secret of the earth and the sky. However, it includes highly sophisticated and reasonable level of occult knowledge. In this volume, you will learn about the lost mind and the knowledge of the lost secrets of our ancient ancestors who were the gods. As long as it is used appropriately, the wisdom that this book offers is good. My honorable spiritual teachers have passed some of this knowledge to me. Therefore, it is my responsibility to expose it to humanity. Such natural and divine duty cause many real spiritual individuals to sacrifice their lives. You have nothing to worry about. This book is intended only as another attempt to induce true awareness into the mind of the people. This ideology is usually the fundamental characteristic of most dangerous books.

Hopefully, you will eventually come to understand that many religions, as well as various forms of government, are purposely designed to keep the mind of people sleeping while they are awake. *The Last Stratum* is not the first attempt intended to eliminate the spell of somnambulism from the mind of the people.

Any book, as well as human being, which stands to stimulate the mind of the people is considered dangerous. For instances, Toussaint Louverture, Mahatma Gandhi, Malcolm X, Nelson Mandela and Martin Luther King were considered as "dangerous" men. Without further ado, let us begin our journey.

Warning: Because this book contains the truth, it may be dangerous. Within the pages of this book, one will come across the truth. Sometimes the truth may be uncomfortable. It may create disturbances in an unprepared mind and lead to mental instability or criminalities. Various adverse effects could be the result of simple misinterpretation of the truth within a fragile mind. The fact is: It does not matter how you feel about the truth. The truth will always remain the truth. It is the only thing that can set your mind free.

Turn the page to begin a real spiritual journey. It will serve as an enjoyable experience and will allow you the opportunity to penetrate deep into the self. Finally, you will be able to explore the mysterious psyche of not only the human mind but also the entire universal mind.

~CHAPTER 4~

Human's Center of Perception
The Brain

THE BRAIN is a superb biological computer. It is equipped with incredible power due to its imagination. Such power allows us to deal delicately with imposed limitations due to space and time. The mind and its imaginary attributes enable you to travel back in forth through space and time without side effects. The human mind has no limitations.

To make progress in this matter, you have to come to the realization that you inherit the mental power of your ancient ancestors, and you came from the ultimate source of creation. This simple change in perception is enough to cause your mind to undertake subtle transformation. As it has been said, "A journey of a thousand miles begins with the first step."

You and everything else in the universe are limitless. A hydrogen atom is made of one proton and one electron. Believe it or not, as of today, despite such simplicity, physicists continue to dispute that a single atom of the simplest element in the universe, hydrogen, is an exceedingly complex piece of matter. Amazingly, after billions of years of evolutionary time, universal intelligence combines billions and billions of protons and electrons in such a manner that they interact harmoniously as a natural, biological network that represents your center of perception.

Unfortunately, we have been constrained to operate within a narrow margin of only seven percent of the totality of this extraordinary network. The imposed limitation is nothing to worry you. Based on universal laws, it has been imposed indiscriminately. Again, due to such induced restriction, most of the human's potential remains dormant. Billions of possible routines and circuit modules remain dormant inside the human's brain. However, if you prepare, train and exercise your brain and your mind, you could accomplish things that would appear to be magical. With enough persistence, you could reactivate dormant connections of your brain to supplement an array of beautiful experiences to your existence.

As mentioned, there are millions of brain circuitries which remain dormant, and they are waiting to be activated. Yes, those circuits existed as natural, survival supplements. They are the small, electrochemical circuits of the brain that scientists recognize as brain cells. After you had been degraded from a godly status to human status, most of your brain circuitries have become inactive. As a result, you become a vulnerable being.

Your vulnerability could be exploited to gradually degrade you down further from a human status to animal status, and so on. Such degradation of the human mind renders you vulnerable to many slick, malicious tricks from certain leading personages who understand quite well the science of the human's spirit, mental limitations and manipulations. They are trying to manipulate your mind to keep you in an elusive form of somnambulism. Their primary goal is to continue to utilize you as a servant to help them achieve their devilish objectives.

It is understood that you have been exposed to religious dogma before, but who has not? Fortunately, today, the existence of various search engines enable you to verify almost anything. After all, you have a brain, a complex biological machine inside your head. It is never a terrible idea to find out about some of its intricacies. Once you fully recognize the capabilities and the power of the human mind, you will know the truth, and you will be free from all bondages. Furthermore, you will be able to better utilize your brain, and you will be, without a doubt, a real son of god.

Neuroscientists have been working incredibly hard to unlock the mysteries of the brain. Amazingly, they have found out that the brain of a healthy, newborn baby has more neuronal connections than that of a healthy adult. Nature has done its part; it has initially provided us with extra brain circuitries just to ensure maximum survival. However, the decaying process has diminished our progress and our capabilities. Once survival and learning become routine, deactivation starts. In other words, the extra neurons die rapidly. That is not because they are no longer needed, but because you do not utilize them. You start losing them at an approximated rate of 114000 neurons per day. The older you are, the more neurons you lose. The less you use your brain, the more neurons you're wasting. Therefore, as one is getting older, his brain works harder to learn new things and to accept new ideas. If you had not been intensively involved in any form of learning activity, you would have determined that it was difficult to learn anything new. Especially, if you had left your mind dormant for too long, it could have become static and required considerable energy to get it back to normal operation.

At a certain point, during old ages, you are only left with the activated neurons. Often, at a particularly early age, the ordinary man's life becomes a routine. The brain does not have the necessity to fire some of its supplemental circuitries anymore. The individual operates as if on automatic control. He no longer has to think carefully. He thinks he has reached his full potential and has no need for new knowledge and creativities. He categorically refuses to continue the process of the development of his brain. If anything requires a little bit of thinking, he becomes upset. In this case, this individual is waiting for death to come. He wastes valuable time complaining about virtual circumstances around him. He personifies the almighty to create justification for his aberration. He would talk about the unfairness of God, the political system, the president and the people. He stops the process of mental refinement. He no longer participates in universal affairs. He remains remarkably static and wants to stop any change, in anything, whatever it may be. He is consciously and unconsciously refusing to adapt. In other words, he is inviting death to rush towards him. The process of dying begins to creep rapidly into his life without realizing it. Therefore, his biological clock is subconsciously accelerated to re-identify him to look like a weak person. In fact, he hopes that others would feel sorry for him. If you do not feel sorry for him, he complains. Believe it or not, he is not someone to have around. Such individual's mind becomes a perfect breeding ground for malicious acts of hatred, racism, prejudice and the like.

The only thing that can keep some brain circuitries from dying is to stimulate and utilize them. You have to keep striking them with new challenges that allow them to stay active. You have to cultivate the strong mentality that death is the only thing that can stop you from going forward. It is best to continue to progress towards the ultimate objective to approach and become the representation of God.

Once a particular activity becomes a routine, it is being processed subconsciously, and the number of neurons involves in the process is reduced considerably. You have to keep the neurons working. Otherwise, the internal programming of the brain is set to assume that they are no longer needed. As a result, the brain is slowly dying.

Death is a universal, natural process. It is what advanced esoteric minds define as the cycle of rebirth. The apparently dying neurons of the brain will be redistributed throughout the universe. This natural process sustains the universal balance and conforms to the manifestation of the natural cycle of life.

However, the plasticity of the brain still retains its ability to duplicate more neurons. As Dr. Deepak Chopra phrased it, "Inside each and every one of us, there is a god in embryo waiting to be born." Remember, the law is the law, and when the law in question identifies one of the universal laws, it cannot be violated.

~CHAPTER 5~

The Teaching of Symmetry
Ancestral Wisdom

IF you decide to do a little search on your own, you would quickly discover not only the bookstores but also the Internet is encumbered with a multitude of materials about the mind and its relation to the brain. One fascinating subject is about how to use both sides of the brain. This teaching is exceptionally interesting. However, the preconceived notion that we have two different brains is not accurate. The inference is that one side of the brain cannot do what the other side can. Here, it seems to exist some serious misunderstanding of the human brain. Before going any further, let us clarify the subject of the two brains.

Behind your skull, you have two powerful biological computers: a left one and a right one. They are physically identical to each other, and they serve as complements to each other. They are what we identify as the brain. They are naturally designed to work together harmoniously as if they were one machine or separately as two different devices. The point is either side of the brain can do what the other side can. However, certain groups or cultures tend to use a particular hemisphere for data processing that is different from some other groups. We use different hemisphere; it all depends on the environment and the culture where we happen to develop. Over time, each brain starts to behave a bit differently. Saying that each side of the brain is different is not an accurate statement. It is like saying each hand, or each eye is made for different purposes or each kidney performs different roles. Human beings are equipped with more than one of certain organs; not because they perform different functions, but because this is the way that nature harmonizes to ensure survival in the human species. If one organ or part of one organ is defective, a person can possibly manage with the other part that is still functioning.

Almost every individual is born with two eyes. If a person loses sight in one eye, he still can use the other eye to help him see and survive. However, this time, he will have to adapt to his new way of seeing things. The eyes are positioned on your face at a slightly different position. Therefore, each eye registers the environment from a different point of view. Each records different images. Then, through a complex biological process, the brain combines the images into one. This magical process allows you to see one single image using two different eyes. In other words, the eyes are complements of each other. Like the brain, they can operate together as one or separately as independent, single, biological, optical instruments. The eyes, working together, create impressive complementary actions. Such actions allow the transmission of beautiful, enhanced, three-dimensional images to the brain to be decoded. This interrelated, advanced signal processing of both eyes and both sides of the brain render an individual's worldview more enjoyable. For instance, if a person loses sight in one eye, he can still see with the other. However, some of the information in his vision would be lost. His view of the world would become less defined, almost flat. During ordinary consciousness, three-dimensional properties of both eyes cannot be reproduced with one physical eye. However, the individual still can see and adapt to his less defined and flat view of his surroundings.

Similarly, the human brain does the same. For instance, if part of one side goes wrong, a person still can use the other to survive the loss. Even though living with only one side is not always possible, it could happen. A person may be paralyzed on one side from head to toe, but it is possible for the plasticity of his brain to reconstruct neuronal circuitries that would help him adapt as if the individual were still whole. However, learning as well as his <u>ranging</u> of consciousness will decrease significantly, depending on the extent of the injury. The active brain is capable of creating alternatives for lost capabilities if it is being challenged.

If you want to use both sides of your brain equally, start to do some exercises. Exercising the brain can help you regain mental balances. Everything you can do with the right side of the body, you try it with the left side as well. Then, you will discover how challenging these basic exercises can be. Keep doing the activity until you become comfortable with either side; until you do not have a favorite side. Some activities would take some time to symmetrize. Of course, this ability was dormant for so long; it may take years to accomplish. For instance, to kick the ball with either foot without preference, some soccer players train both of their feet. The development of such ability qualifies them as first-rank players. They do not have a preferred side. Left or right, it does not matter from which direction the ball is coming, they can capture it to develop quick strategies. On the other hand, a non-symmetrized player would be a bit slow if the ball happens to reach him on the dormant side.

You can start symmetrizing your brain with some ball juggling, which is extremely beneficial to improve coordination. See how difficult it is to juggle two balls with either hand. A good exercise is to try writing with the left hand. If you are left handed, try to write with the right hand. Change your computer's mouse from a right-handed configuration to a left-handed configuration and vice versa. Whatever sport you play, train your other side equally until you become a whole-brained player, with the same level of comfort on either side. If you can do just that, you will notice that a non-symmetrized player is a no-match to you. Your body's ability, flexibility and reflex will improve considerably. Also, your ability to play sports, your speed, and your sense of spatial position in relation to other objects will enhance significantly. It is a natural law that movements and body motions alter the brain's electro-chemical circuitries.

You do not have to believe in this teaching. ***The Last stratum*** is a purely scientific thinking. Do some experiment yourself and enjoy the end results. Try anything you used to do with one side of the body, do it with the opposite side. Start with something as essential as brushing your teeth, writing, eating, whatever, and you are on your way to becoming a new symmetrized being. These simple exercises can transform you in ways that you never thought possible. The secret of physical symmetry is one of the secrets of the ancient teachings of the gods.

~CHAPTER 6~

The Law of Universal Balance
Conservation of Energy

THE LAW of Universal Balance is imposed in a sense that you cannot acquire something for nothing. Within the scientific community, it is identified as the law of Conservation of Energy. This law states that energy cannot be created nor destroyed. Therefore, energy can only be converted from one form to another. In a sense, while you are consuming some kind of energy from the universe, you are giving it back in different ways. You may not recognize the outcome because it usually transforms. This law is strictly enforced to preserve the harmonious balance of nature. Whatever the circumstance, this interchanging process is happening. It never stops, and it never fails to occur. The simple act of trying to "take away" something from the universe without giving something else back, could be deadly. You cannot impede universal laws. They have been in place before time. Do not ever try to violate these laws. It is categorically impossible to alter and amend universal laws (The Last Stratum, Volume II).

The simplest way to be aware of the law of Universal Balance is to cut your breathing by holding your nose. Only a professional diver or someone who trains to hold his breath can hold on for more than two minutes. Otherwise, he has to let go quickly. The ordinary man cannot hold his breath for more than a minute or so. When you inhale you take air from the universe into your body. This seemingly simple process is significantly complex. However, it is extremely vital. It allows the body to transform bits of matter into energy. On the other hand, when you exhale, you are releasing carbon dioxide into the universe. Air serves as energy to the human body while carbon dioxide provides energy to the plants and other living forms.

Your body transforms the food you eat and the liquids you drink into bones, enzymes, brain cells, organs and the like. After processing, food exits your body as "wastes" such as grease, sweat, urine and feces. They are also essential for the soil and different forms of life. If you try to stop this natural process, you would only hurt yourself. When proper universal exchanges are combined with exercises such as yoga training and certain mental rituals, they create the state of natural symmetry, balance and serenity within an individual's body and mind. Physical and psychological balances are directly related; one can certainly stimulate the other.

The universe is an exceedingly complex field; it is too complicated for the ordinary mind to comprehend it all. Do not try to understand all the details of this introductory teaching. If you cannot understand something immediately, do not worry about it. However, If you honestly want to understand this teaching, you have to spend time pondering on it for a while or for a long time, if necessary. You must be willing to step in and get wet. It is understood that some of this teaching is too advanced for the ordinary mind. It is important to realize that every talent or skill to develop often requires a tremendous amount of practice. The key is practice, practice, and continue to practice. The earlier you start, the better. This teaching is not discouraging to prevent older people from trying. Anyone can do it; however, a child can progress faster. You ask, why? A child has sixteen hours a day, and his mind is young. In other words, a child's mind is in the process of being programmed. An adult, on the other hand, has only two hours or less a day, and his mind has already been programmed. Of course, an adult's mind can be reprogrammed. However, it requires considerable effort, time and energy. As a result, old minds are challenging to train and reprogram. They are already conditioned, and they tend to resist changes.

As mentioned, you have at your disposal billions of brain circuitries waiting for an eventual activation. When you undertake mental practices, you are allowing a few dormant circuits of the brain to be reactivated. In a sense, the brain becomes more involved, using new neuronal connections, and it is automatically using more of itself. Therefore, the goddess within you is slowly waking up. Some of the blocked memories are starting to reappear. Your mind will be free from the traditional system of belief. You will be unrestricted of conditional limitations. That will allow you to think clearly and creatively. A combined physical and mental preparation could take you to appropriate octave of mind and balance that you would have never thought possible. This is what happens to magicians, professional athletes, draughts and chess players, dancers, circus performers, yogis, voodoo priests, Zen masters, shamans, and the like. Through years of rituals and practices, the brain allows specific, dormant neuronal circuitries to reactivate.

For instance, the new sense of reality that some of the spiritual masters acquire is not automatic. They are obtained through a variety of rituals and exercises such as transcendental meditation, visualization, imagination, hypnotism, chanting, breathing, walking, martial arts, running, yoga and the like. These are some of the rituals that allow the grand masters to increase their senses of reality. In other terms, they can expand the abilities of the mind to perceive reality from a different perspective without side effects. And sometimes they reach the ultimate point where they can no longer understand ordinary people. If you have patience and the desire to practice, you can acquire these same levels of power. It is all up to you. Also, you must understand that these great masters are not equipped with supernatural powers that come from thin air.

The great power they have is available to anyone willing to pay a high price.

The brain is capable of increasing your abilities and sense of reality that you may think come from some supernatural power. The real master never fails to believe that the power he has is available to anyone who is willing to train his body and mind.

Once you manage to get a few of those dormant circuits connected, your brain is immediately stimulated. The more circuits you manage to plug in, the better. You can do what the masters do. Hidden sources of universal energy become available to your senses, and you can tap into them to create your personal, independent reality. You can increase your sense of sight, hearing, smell, touch, taste and reflexes. You can also reclaim loss abilities of the brain such as intuition, telepathy, echolocation, and the like. Furthermore, you can take control over most of the involuntary actions of your body; the sky is the limit. It is your body after all. It belongs to you, and you have all of its rights.

Scientists and psychologists have been investigating the potential of the human mind for a long time. As a result, they have developed many experiments to help them find the truth. They have stumbled on biofeedback as recent evidence of our hidden, mental abilities. Psychologists have amazingly discovered that using biofeedback most patients are capable of controlling the involuntary actions of their hearts. Those patients can increase and decrease their heartbeats significantly with no consequences. In many occasions, some yogis have not only reinforced but also demonstrated such mental abilities.

On April 26, 1956, at the All-India Institute of Mental Health in Bangalore, India, the Yogi Shri S. R. Khrishna Iyengar, left a group of scientists, doctors and psychologists with their lower jaws dropped. He stayed for over nine hours in a small underground compartment containing only one cubic meter of air. To their amazement, Shri wanted to stay for a day and a half in the chamber, but the scientists believed that nine hours are more than enough. No ordinary human can stay underground for more than nine hours, living on such small portion of only one cubic meter of air. It is a feat that requires significant conditioning of the mind and the body.

Again, during the year 1970 many experiments with Swami Rama, an Indian yogi, proved that he could increase his heart rate up to 300 beats a minute. We now know for sure that the mind and the body are directly related. Therefore, a changing mind creates a changing being. You can customize your perception beyond the average human limitation, and bring it close to that of an imaginable being. Through the therapeutic effects of rituals, mantra, imagination, meditations, music and diet, nothing is impossible!

There is a real story about a young musician. Evelyn Glenny started to lose her hearing at a young age to the point that she could not hear anymore. She learned to read lips, and she developed a different sense of hearing. The vibration of the instrument she is playing tells her which note she plays. Remarkably, her brain transforms touchable vibration into sound. This may seem like nonsense to unscientific individuals. However, scientifically sound produces material vibrations, and material vibrations produce sounds. In other terms, she can touch the vibrating instrument to determine the note it produces. She is no longer relying on her sense of hearing to hear. Amazingly, she reconfigures her brain to convert the sense of touch into the sense of hearing. This makes perfect sense. Scientifically speaking, the number of vibrations per second is what determines the note plays by an instrument. In fact, many animals, insects as well as mammals make use of vibratory communications. For instances, deers, rats and mice are capable of detecting danger of approaching predators from a distance due to mechanical vibrations. Most insects in addition to snakes utilize physical vibrations extensively to identify prey and attract mates.

Bats are small mammals that prefer to live in the dark. They are social animals. In other words, they learn to live in-group, usually in large, dark caves. Bats are nocturnal species. Therefore, they sleep in the daytime and go out after sunset to look for food. A bat cave can contain more than a million bats. It is a wonder to observe how bats are flying in a closed pack without colliding with each other. Bats do have eyes; however, they do not use them much. Because they cannot see in the dark, they use a navigational system that scientists called echolocation to navigate in the darkest caves. They emit a variety of ultra high frequency sounds, not audible to human ear. As they emit a series of high-frequency pulses, their ears capture the echo. The echo is processed by their tiny brains to create three-dimensional images of their environment. Bats are adapted to this form of navigation; their brains forget almost completely about how to use visual senses. So, they utilize their ears to see and hunt for food. Therefore, eliminate the needs to rely on their eyes when navigating in the dark. Their eyes are ineffective in the dark.

Many cave creatures do not have eyes. They dwell in the dark; therefore, they do not need eyes. They use vibrations, sounds and echo to find their ways. Other animals such as dolphins and whales also use echolocation to communicate and to find their ways in obscure water. The question is: If the world plunges into darkness, could humanity manage to utilize echolocation? The answer is: Yes, but not immediately. Human has such hidden potential; it only needs to be redeveloped. The problem is we have lost this exceptional ability, and the brain completely forgets about it. This is because we, humans, have been using our eyes at birth. The existence and the abundance of light make it exceedingly difficult to develop this ancient, mental ability.

The next chapter will open a small window into the power of suggestions. It will take you through an amazing story about a young boy under his mother's suggestions reconfigures his brain to utilize echolocation.

~CHAPTER 7~

The Story of a Human Bat

Mental Reconfiguration

AFTER a doctor visit with his mother, the three-year-old boy was diagnosed with eye cancer. The doctor declared that both eyes had been infected. Then he said, "For the child to survive," he shrugged desperately," I have to remove both of his eyes. Otherwise, this form of cancer will spread rapidly and attack his brain and internal organs." The doctor insisted for a decision to be made as soon as possible. The boy's mother was crushed. She did not know what to do and was not too far from losing her mind. Her motherly love and passion were too much to let go of her son. Trapped between two evils, she had to decide. She agreed with the doctor for the eyes of her beloved son to be removed. At least, he will still be alive. Some people thought it would be better to let the boy dies. Soon after the surgery, the boy started to complain. He said, "Mom I can't see anything! I will not be able to do anything!" The mother responded, "What do you mean, you will not be able to do anything?" The boy replied, "I can't see anything Mom!" Mother felt powerless. She knew already that her son could not see, but the lamentation of her son was cutting through her heart. She was under unbearable mental stress; she did not know what to answer. As the boy continued to complain about not being able to see, she reacted. She was about to tell Ben to stop complaining. However, in a suggestive, loving tone of voice, she said, "What do you mean? Your name is Ben; you will be able to do anything you want! You will be able to drive a car if you want to!" These are, in fact, some incredibly powerful suggestions. She reacted positively to the stress of the moment. However, she did not seriously believe that her blind son would be able to do anything he wants. Unknowingly, she applied the hidden power of positive suggestion. The effect is: Young children firmly believe in their mothers' suggestions. For every child of this age, his mother's words are the words of God. For that matter, every three-year-old boy or girl exists in a reality of a state of mind where he/she can easily be programmed and reprogrammed. You can make them believe anything, provided that they have trust in you. In fact, it is not only young children that you can make believe anything. Unleashing the power of your mind, you can make almost anyone, if not everyone, believes anything. In practice, however, it is a little bit more difficult, but it is possible.

Let us continue with our story. About a year after the operation, the boy started to make a series of clacking sounds with his mouth. His mother did not know why he was making them, but she paid him no mind. She noticed that the boy could find his way around the house without stumbling and touching like ordinary blind people. She was amazed when she had learned from a specialist that her son was using bat communications (echolocation) to find his way around.

Ben and his mother came to the Oprah's show. The boy was capable of walking alone in the street or anywhere without a cane. He was also capable of distinguishing between different types of materials such as metal, glass, and wood. He said that echo from various materials sounds different. Ben was capable of riding a skateboard down the street like any ordinary kid. Ben was sixteen years old when he appeared on the Oprah's show with his mother.

We may apparently think of him as an exception; however, he is not. He is only using the hidden power of the human mind to compensate for his handicap. Echolocation is one of the lost capabilities of the human mind. Despite the difficulty involves in regaining lost abilities of the human mind, any blind three-year-old with a healthy brain can learn to use echolocation. We are quick to condition others to make them believe that they are limited. As a result, we make it almost impossible for our youths to reactivate dormant brain circuitries. Many of them prove us wrong. Ben is the living proof of the power of positive suggestions and the human's mind. If it were not for those early suggestions from Ben's mother, Ben would have never been the kid he is. A mother is the most influential figure for a child. Consequently, mother's suggestions to her children contain as much power as the words of God. At a remarkably early age, your mother is your god. Her suggestions can affect your mind, your body, and you soul.

Although we have lost the fundamental privilege to operate on the same level of consciousness as the gods, our ability to become god again has not been entirely lost. It is still there dormant within every single one of us. However, it is up to us to make the decision to become god again.

When you educate yourself to regain some of the hidden abilities of the human mind, you are gradually transforming into a new and more advanced being. Your awareness may develop unexpectedly. Through observation, rituals, imagination, music and diet, you can achieve the maximum potential of mental strength. You can practice thinking, seeing and sensing similar to an imaginary entity. You can be a spiritual being with attributes that you establish yourself. You can transform into a god of communication, of love, of beauty, of peace, and of compassion. You can become the individual you always dreamed of being. You can be anything you want, provided you honestly want something. You can use your practices and rituals to match your personal reality.

Many things that you consider impossible are because you have been deprived of the knowledge to understand them. With constant improvement, all impossibilities will transform into real possibilities right under your nose.

"If we did not invent the word impossible, everything would have probably been possible." What you must remember is that: The perception of impossibilities is nothing but negative awareness of human's lower level of consciousness.

The field of knowledge is not only extensive and obscure, but it is also exciting. However, people have a strong tendency to apply advanced knowledge without regards to the simple fact that knowledge is always a double-sided sword. It is neither good nor evil, but it can be good or evil. Many have fallen into delusion to believe that the knowledge at hand is absolute. Therefore, negative perception of advanced knowledge is reinforced. For all knowledge, there exists finer and more advanced knowledge than what you already know. As you are being absorbed by the experience of true mind, and the universal knowledge of the ancients, deep, deep, deep, at a specific level of consciousness, you will inadvertently experience the power of universal unification. Furthermore, you will no longer be able to make a clear distinction of your professed reality. At that level of mindfulness, all extremities and oppositions would merge. For instance, past and present, life and death, good and evil, love and hate, beautiful and ugly, light and dark, hot and cold would be all mingling into one. At that point, you may not even be aware of your subtle curving toward the infinite field of mind, which is the mind of god. This feeling is as if a magnetic and supernatural form of energy is guiding you in the direction of your originality. You are eventually free to enter the consciousness of god. Your mind is now open and ready to perform in a godlike fashion. You have crossed the line of demarcation, and you can no longer return. You are freeing yourself from all bondages of mind. You have just unconsciously guided into the field of esoteric knowledge of your ancestors who were the gods.

Warning: ***The Last Stratum*** is the realm of the transformation of human consciousness. Therefore, this publication is not for everyone. Remember you are now entering ***THE LAST STRATUM***, the dimension of forbidden fields of advanced knowledge of the mind. As mentioned, your mind must be prepared.

The next chapter will take you deeper into the field of infinite and universal consciousness.

~CHAPTER 8~

The Ultimate Consciousness
Higher Level of Being

The truth will illuminate the darkness of the mind and carry the power to create your own universe.
Guirand Michel

A MODEST observation of ourselves could bring the realization that we are the most intelligent beings ever existed on this planet. As humans, we are gifted with unique, unlimited mind power. Therefore, we are obviously not ordinary animals. However, some individuals strongly disagree with this viewpoint. A discussion with Mr. John, a new friend at a bookstore in Fort Lauderdale, Florida, exposed some amazing ideas.

Mr. John argued, "We perceived to be different from the animals' kingdom. Such error in judgment is nothing but poor mental misinterpretations. The earth and everything on it deserve protection, admiration, love and respect. The animals are not exceptions. We are nothing better than a small ant. To be capable of respecting the animals, we must first come to accept the fact that we are also animals. Unfortunately, our unintelligent, negative perception of being superior will eventually lead us, human beings, towards total destruction.

Such complex of superiority was the result of the Spanish destroyed the native people of America. Under that same negative perception of being superior, the Portuguese, the French, the British, the Americans and the Arabs made the largest criminal attempted in history to destroy the black race of Africa. An average of six hundred million innocent, African men and women lost their lives. The aberration of superiority leads the spirit of man to contemplate malicious ideologies such as racism, prejudice, and discrimination. It is this psychological delusion that drove Hitler to kill six million Jews people, so on and so forth. The belief of superiority is delusional, stupid and irrational. It desensitizes the mind and could lead to criminality. Common sense tells you that divine superiority does not involve killing and destroying everything and everyone that look different. On the contrary, it is a radiant spectrum of understanding, compassion, unity and love for everything and everyone whatever the differences."

Mr. John continued, "Obviously, men are progressing in a way totally opposed to the will of the gods. Man's deviation from the original mind of the gods creates the complex case of the state of mental inferiority that makes him believe that he is superior to others. Therefore, he is mentally trapped in the complex convolution of mind. He is striving to prove his superiority over others. In this desperate attempt, he subconsciously displays his frustrations as a compulsive desire to eliminate differences. He becomes aberrant and irrational. He takes pride in winning wars as well as killing and destroying other races and innocent people that have nothing to do with him. Through devilish objectives, he exploits and murders everything different from him. He is destroying not only the human race but also the planet earth and himself. His ferocious attitude breeds the multiplication of violence, hate and suffering. It is sad to observe how human beings are carelessly ravaging our precious planet. They are unconsciously destroying themselves, and demonstrate an absolute disregard for life. Man feels superior and advanced, but he cannot perceive the underlying fact that he is still living at the mercy of the natural forces. Truly, Human beings are ferocious animals. In most instances, they prefer killing rather than helping and forgiving. Many governments are addicted to killing. They choose to spend billions of dollars creating all kinds of deadly weapons of war. Consequently, our beautiful, innocent women, men and children around the world are unnecessarily dying of diseases and starvation. Human beings are destroying everything! I mean everything!"

Then Mr. John briefly stopped for a while, as if to catch a breath and exclaimed, "Progressing in that direction will, without a doubt, bring our own destruction." Then making a miserable sigh, he deeply inhaled and exhaled while shaking his head from side to side, with frustration.

I patiently listened to Mr. John's arguments with passion. After his declaration, out of compassion, I decided to take a close look at him. I noticed not only his face but also his eyes were all red, indicating that he was extremely upset. His discourse resonated as if it is a cry out for help.

Some of Mr. John's arguments reflect on various scientific researches on animal behavior of different species. Some people used to believe that human is nothing but a predator animal that would kill and fight to defend his territories. However, more investigation on the subject has proven otherwise. Scientists from around the world have united to study and discuss the issue of human behavior. On May 16, 1986, in Seville, Spain, they established and signed the "Seville Statement on Violence" indicating that it is scientifically incorrect to state that violent behavior is genetically programmed in human nature. Therefore, the evil tendency to make war, kill, torture, and destroy without proper causes was not originally programmed into the human mind. Scientists did not ignore the fact that humans have the ability to react in accordance with the environment. However, excessive violence is not automatic; it is not natural to be violent in most situations. Violent people are suffering from psychosomatic derangement.

Again, during a discussion with Mr. Joe X, a graduate from Wentworth Institute of Technology in Boston, he argued that human activities do not prove signs of intelligence, but, rather, signs of negative, destructive behavior. He pointed out slavery and wars as the lowest form of human degradation. Mr. Joe X argued that humans possess a kind of negative behavior that is out to destroy the earth. This statement showed that Mr. Joe refused to accept human's activities as signs of superior intelligence. He rather described human's behavior as "negative intelligence". Therefore, his view falls parallel with Mr. John's.

At the end of this interesting dialogue, I looked at Mr. Joe as if he was the reincarnation of Mr. John. Then, I reacted with a superior attitude, and I said, "Negative intelligence is nothing other than intelligence." Mr. Joe looked at me for a moment, quiet, with a serious manner and squinted eyes. Rubbing his lips together while biting on them and replied, "Would you take a negative two for a two?" I could not respond, for I realized that I was undoubtedly faced with an intelligent personality.

It seems obvious that we are also animals, but it is evident that we are the most intelligent beings on earth. We may think this is the traditional belief. However, personalities such as Mr. Joe and Mr. John believe otherwise. They have made some good points. However, this introductory teaching of *The Last Stratum* does not advocate that. Various religions and ancient manuscripts taught us to accept and to recognize human being as the most intelligent creature on earth. We have learned from various, ancient scriptures that "God" created man in his image and gave him dominion over all things. However, looking back at our continuing behavior over time shows how much human has abused his domination right.

He continues to use his delusional superiority to behave in a fashion that the gods were not intended.

After all, we must accept that our original minds become conditioned and infected with negative influences. However, operating on a higher level of conscious will help us develop a better understanding. Higher octave of consciousness could help us filter various forms of malicious tendencies that interfere with our original nature. To do this, we must first start with an investigation of our center of consciousness. Although it represents the axis of all of our psychological sufferings such as anxieties, resentments, hatreds, miseries and all kinds of confusions, it is also the master lock with the secret combinations that will open the door to mental liberation.

This teaching is simply another attempt to recalibrate the human mind and to slowly guide man toward previous, godlike consciousness. Self-expression, beauty, health, happiness, intelligence, logic and reasoning are fractional derivatives of an individual's consciousness. You cannot change any of these factors without first altering an individual state of awareness. You will understand that as you progress further; you must keep an open mind. For, the truth is an essential component of knowledge that contains the power to transcend ordinary consciousness.

~CHAPTER 9~

The Effects of Memory
Amnesic Induction

Knowledge and awareness carry the solution to every condition.
 Guirand Michel

THE OBJECTIVE of this teaching is to help you bypass the difficulties imposed by your conditioned memory partitions. This will create access channels to your true memory and help you on your journey to cultivate your abilities as the son of god. However, due to evolutionary time, what you truly were is hidden deep beneath many layers of mental strata. The only way to become what you were is to break through the conditioned memory partitions that re-identified and separated you from your ancient ancestors who were the gods. You are the creation and the image of the gods. You have hidden in yourself all the powers and characteristics of a god.

Due to these large partitions of conditioned memories that obstruct your mind, your divine consciousness remains dormant. Therefore, you may not be aware of the power that you own. You are living in a dormant state of mind. However, the slightest awareness of your original state could be considered as the seed that will grow toward the development of your divine consciousness.

Is it possible to regain divine consciousness? How can I remember what happened millions of years ago?

You must understand that nothing is impossible, and all impossibilities are negative awareness of lower levels of consciousness. Therefore, they could easily be transformed into actual possibilities. Yes, you have been created in the image and the likeness of the gods. You are the son of god; therefore, you are also a god. However, you just forgot the time when you were a god. Your dormant mind is operating in an amnesiac state. Do not blame yourself for that. You forget what you ate for dinner yesterday; you cannot remember what you did last Wednesday. You just opened the door with your key, then, you forgot the key in the door lock. You have just worn your hat, and you are looking for it while it is over your head. Amazingly, you are looking for your glasses, while you are wearing them. How can you remember what you were billions of years ago?

In fact, billions of years ago, the outcome of your materialization was only a probability function. To barely start scratching the surface, it requires that we put ourselves in shape through rigorous mental training, education, and diet. With that, hopefully, we will eventually end up dispelling partitions of conditioned memories that our minds have been feeding on for a long time. Although it is certainly attainable, it is not going to be easy. The result may not reach full expectation without your full determination. Trying to remember and to become what you were billions of years ago are extremely complicated feats of memory manipulation. They are not possible without a fundamental switch and total revolution in consciousness.

The true you is buried under a heavy load of a countless number of conditioned memory strata. Therefore, you mistakenly identify yourself with the conditioned memories instead of the true, real memory of yourself. This misidentification results because the conditioned memories you evaluate yourself with are closer to you in conscious time than the true, original memory of yourself. This is because of the way your conscious mind organizes time. Although real time is naturally curved with space, when you are fully awake, your ordinary, conscious mind rearranged time into a simple model of linear patterns. This is to protect your conditioned, conscious mind from total confusion. However, your subconscious mind does not allow such limitation. It keeps time curved. Therefore, the subconscious mind does not distort true time; it keeps it curved, as it should be. This property allows the subconscious mind to have access to distant events in time.

In conscious time, one hour earlier is closer to you than yesterday. Yesterday is closer to you than last month. Last month is closer to you than last year and so on and so forth. As time goes by, in the conscious plane, the furthest memories are faded into distant, linear spacetime continuum. Such constant, linear flow of time creates the effect of natural, universal amnesia. As a result, you can remember what happened to you one hour earlier, but you cannot remember what happened to you last week, last month, last year, or the last decade with the same degree of accuracy. As time flows through your conscious mind and seems to pass you by in a linear pattern, the furthest memories fade away in relation with spacetime throughout the vast, infinite spacetime dimension. However, the closest conditioned memory field remains clear. This effect is due to conscious spacetime dissociation. It is not only one of the most captivating illusions of the human mind, but it is also one of the most natural and confusing effects of the conscious mind. This illusory effect of time gave birth to the following conscious law, stating that: "The position in space and time of any entity in relation to the position in space and time of its observer determines its definition to the observer." This law works great on the conscious level. For instances, suppose you are standing a few feet from a vehicle. Then, someone starts it and drives it away from you. As time and space are changing between you and the vehicle, the definition and the size of the vehicle are also changing until you can no longer see the vehicle. Its instances look different at every integral moment in time. The vehicle gradually appears to fade away into linear spacetime until your physical senses can no longer receive the transmitted information (color, size and sound) from the vehicle. As a result, it disappears into the distance. Because you cannot see the vehicle, that does not mean that it does not exist; it still exists at a particular position in space and time. However, because of the curvature of spacetime, your ordinary senses cannot receive transmitted information from the vehicle anymore. On the contrary, your subconscious memory is capable of keeping time curved. Therefore, it helps you retain a clear, mental image of the vehicle.

Now imagine you can observe a stationary vehicle for a lifetime. You can see that the vehicle is changing right under your nose. As spacetime varies, not only the vehicle is changing, it is also transforming. This property of spacetime also enclosed the law of transformation. The perception of distant events is different from that of events nearby. This is not only because of the limitations of our physical senses, but it is also due to the structure of spacetime.

From that point on, you are equipped with enough information. You should be able to realize that conscious observation of space and time is a complex, distorted effect due to limitations of the ordinary conscious mind.

An average man, by default, identifies himself with the closest, conditioned memory partitions in reference to conscious observation in spacetime. Consequently, when memory exists in a distant past, the ordinary man is in trouble. He is unaware of it because he has no way of accessing it. He cannot access ancient memories, using the regular, conscious plane. Therefore, in his usual quest for identification, man has no choice but to identify himself with what he can remember. What he can remember is nothing but a gradient stack of the closest, conditioned memories. If these memory partitions form a stack of nonsenses, he is automatically identified himself as such. The funny thing about that is, he is incapable to see and to detect where his nonsensical personality comes from. So, he completely ignores and forgets about the true him. Again, this is not his fault. His real identity is deteriorated into a distant past.

Billions of years may appear to be a long time to the conscious mind. As mentioned, these distant chunks of time are not accessible on the conscious level. With severe mental education, it becomes possible to access most of these lost memories through the subconscious plane. Again, the reason is at subconscious level spacetime is not only linear it is also curved. Therefore, distant past-memories could be as obvious as yesterday's memories.

The perception of time in ordinary consciousness is illusive, as of everything else. Normal consciousness makes a small amount of time appears to be incredibly vast. In a curved spacetime continuum, distant events could be as stimulating as yesterday's experience. The confusion lies within two major abstract components of reality, which are memory and consciousness. To understand the effects of consciousness on time, think about these.

You are in your bedroom lying down on your bed. You just had a long day, and you are trying to relax. Without your awareness, your mind automatically switches into a different mode of consciousness (The Last Stratum, Volume II). Your eyes close. Then, your alarm clock goes off, and you open your eyes. You take a glimpse at the time. Amazingly, eight or more hours have already been passed without your being aware of that. Now you feel refreshed. You quickly take a shower, and you drive to the office to meet with your manager. On arrival, you find out that the manager is busy. He tells you to wait for six hours. Imagine how long six hours can be. Spending six hours doing nothing in ordinary consciousness is not only annoying, but it is also an absolute torture. A slight difference in perception is enough to redefine time completely. During athletic sports, basketball, for example, the winning team perceives the passage of time as being extremely slow, while the losing team believes that time is running too fast. Each team has a different perception as to how long is a three-minute play. This distortion of time affects not only the members of each team, but it also affects the fans. During sports competition, you must have experienced time distortion in that manner. The mental state of the players could also distort the perception of time; however, time is evidently not the same for each team. This is another example of what is called time dilatation. Three minutes for players in the winning team is not equal to three minutes for players in the losing team. Therefore, three minutes is not equal to three minutes. Furthermore, small children and animals do not perceive time as we do. One week is a long time for a dog. Likewise, an animal such as a dog cannot wait five minutes for its food or anything else for that matter.

If you have a dog, do this little experiment. Wait until it is hungry and requesting its plate. First, let your pet dog sees its plate with food in it, and then you tell it to wait. Warning! This simple experiment may upset the dog considerably, but it will not hurt it permanently. If you keep doing this experiment with the same dog, that will finally teach the dog, slowly, how to adapt to human's new concept of time. However, it is not recommended to keep displeasing your dog or any other animals, for that matter. Keep upsetting your dog may cause unpredictable consequences on the behavior of your dog. If you want to do this experiment, do it only once. And, you must consider yourself lucky you cannot understand dog curses. Asking your dog to wait for such a long time that your conditioned, conscious brain defines as "minute" is an abomination. Dogs would not play that. They would howl, bark and talk about your mother. Animals do not define time the same way we do. They are operated in a different state of consciousness. Therefore, in animal perceptions one "human-minute" is defined as a long time.

The human mind can influence time in ways that you would have never thought possible. The mind can move forward and backward into time. Time has no direction, and Albert Einstein has proved that mathematically. The mind seems to exist in perfect accordance with Einstein's theory of relativity. The unconscious mind can leap into past-time memories. This form of memory jump can only be done in the unconscious plane. One does not know or remember when he has made such leaping into time.

We will continue to remind you of your inherent power until all uncertainties of mind are removed from your default awareness. We aim at a high standard. You must remember, although your normal consciousness and your sub-consciousness operate on different frequencies or octaves, they are still related to each other. Consequently, they can influence each other. Therefore, the teaching of *The Last Stratum* is based on this fact to liberate your conscious mind and its intellect from adjacent and persistent conditioned memory partitions. Through reminding you over and over, you will allow yourself to not only examine the idea but also to question it. Then you will start to think about it. Thinking freely will inadvertently filter the truth and let it sink into your subconscious mind. During this process, the conscious intellect is responsible for questioning the truth. The mere act of questioning the truth is incredibly powerful. It is even more significant when you are questioning, and depending only on your intellectual mind to help you find the answer. Consequently, you are forced to engage in your own spiritual expedition. Questioning the truth induced thinking and thinking stimulates your mind. Then, mental stimulation induces visualization, and visualization brings up your accepted reality. Et voilă!

An accepted reality is not necessarily an absolute reality, as many people tend to believe. It carries with it some confusion and sometimes enormous frustrations. Often it resulted in different degrees of perceptions from one individual mind to another. However, if the accepted reality is based on the truth, it is powerful enough to gradually readjust and guide the ordinary mind to true consciousness.

You must concentrate; that is crucial. You will be reprogrammed to be you again. And that is through attempting the utilization of a powerful, mental trick that will ingeniously induce upon you the controlling power to gradually tune yourself to a higher degree of consciousness. If, by any chance, you did not know that you own that kind of power, do not worry. Nobody believes he does.

You are reading **The Last Stratum**. It contains various occult and lost secrets of the mind that have not been exposed to the ordinary man. These secret, spiritual teachings have been kept secret to prevent you from displaying your godlike characteristics. Therefore, you have been passively accepting to live the poorest conditions imaginable that confines you into ignorance and confusion. You will soon discover the inherited power of the mind of your ancient ancestors who were the gods. These ancient secrets of the gods have been taught to selected personages, and that was a long time ago. Part of this teaching is being exposed to you for the first time. Make sure to pay total attention and keep an open mind.

Human's default awareness is calibrated in the range of the beta field of consciousness. Such substandard field of consciousness allows harmonic interferences and logical errors to accumulate as to become part of human's natural perceptions. Those negative mental interferences are one of the leading causes of misidentification. They cause the human mind to experience a distorted reality that leads to various kinds of nonsense such as disorientations, confusions, low self-esteem, hatreds, and frustrations. Therefore, it becomes extremely difficult for the ordinary man to experience the mind of god. On the other hand, it is probable for the mind of man to approach the mind of god. Although it may require a long time, it is indeed possible.

However, the power of readjusting to true consciousness will liberate your mind from various negative influences. Such readjustment of mind will allow you to voluntarily bypass your conditioned memory stacks. Then, you will be free from all bondages of mind, which trap you in to believe something entirely different from the real you. Your whole world will be transforming into something you would never imagine.

Remember, the truth will always remain the truth. It will force itself through you as the truth. The truth is like a source of light in the dark. You can choose to ignore it, but it is remaining as the guide that will allow you to find your way. Every bit of truth carries with it some degree of influence capable to gradually transform the human mind.

You are just beginning to enter the field of *The Last Stratum*. It is the realm of a superior dimension of mind that exists in your psyche as the reality of the gods.

You must understand that the complexity of the material is overwhelming. Keep calm. Do not be discouraged nor be afraid. Anyway, there is absolutely nothing to fright you. Armed with this knowledge, is the key to help you understand who you are. You have been pulling away from your originality for so long. Now is the time to reclaim your right. Utilizing the mental power of your ancestors is your right to become god again. Of course, no one can deny you that. You have the right to redeem your right, and that right is in perfect accordance with the objective of god. You may continue to question and never cease to wonder

The memory partitions that you acquire during your lifetime are your personal memories. They are the products of your living experiences. They form the conditioned boundaries that stop you from experiencing your true self. Universal Memory starts since the beginning of the creation of the universe; it is a component of spacetime. As soon as the universe started to develop, time, space and memory are also formed, and they coexisted together as one. You cannot have one without the others. Universal Memory is also a component of yourself. Even though you can access it at a particular level of consciousness, it is often difficult for the average man to do so. Such dilemma is due to various partitions of conditioned memories. Thus, the ordinary man is an exact instance of his conditioned memories, someone with a false identification of himself. Completely blinded from the truth, he cannot make undistorted distinctions between the real and the unreal. He often perceives the unreal as the real and the real as the unreal. He is being induced into zombie-like condition. An individual in such a situation lacks serious mental stability. He can easily be conditioned to accept anything. He is deprived of his personal, mental power. He is susceptible to follow, accept and execute malevolent wishes of others. Unsecure of himself, he surrenders all of his godly power. He accepts to live in the poorest circumstance of mind as if it were his normal condition. He will defend neither himself nor his people. In a sense, he has the specific characteristics that the elite societies are motivated to find. He is perfect to carry their dirt bags.

The previous declarations are not intended to fright you. However, it is imperative not to leave you in the dark. Without knowledge of certain circumstances, it is impossible to protect against them. After the human mind had been calibrated to operate within the beta dimension of consciousness, it has not been able to see reality, as it should. The ordinary man has, unfortunately, become a zombie.

The trick of the "devil" is to make sure that your mental activities are locked into the beta field of consciousness. As a result, you will remain his slave forever. He is malicious. Without compassion, He exploits the predicaments of his fellow man. Through various mental manipulations and techniques, he reconditions your mind to reject those who accept the challenge to make you aware of your current situation. You have been similarly turned into a zombie that an immoral voodoo priest keeps in the dark. He feeds his zombies special, prepared food to keep them from regaining awareness of their conditions. He reconstructs their memories utilizing drugs and hypnotic rituals. He instructs them to hide and run away from their families and friends to avoid disclosure.

The next chapter will take you into the secret world of Voodoo. It will reveal some of the guarded secrets that have been practiced for thousands of years among the voodoo masters of Africa and Haiti. You will gain a profound understanding of the so-called "Zombification System".

~CHAPTER 10~

Ancient Secrets

Zombification

ZOMBIES live under the absolute control of the voodoo priest. He is capable of having them to do anything he wishes. He exploits and abuses them; he often forces them into slavery. Believe it or not, he does not have to chain his zombies. Once their personal memory collections are blocked, they have no choice but to form and to adopt new ones. Therefore, they have no personal memories to identify with except the recently induced memory bank that the Voodoo Priest creates for them. They immediately become an instance of that induced memory. As a result, zombies are not capable to either return home, or to fight for their rights. They are suffering a form of induced amnesia. You can fight for them if you want to, but they are not going to help you. They could, however, turn against you if they have been instructed to do so. If you seriously want to fight for them, you would have to remove them from the terrible environmental condition that they have been put through. Furthermore, using a form of re-education, you would also have to change their regular diet, have them exercise and teach them the truth. Hopefully, slowly they will recover.

Many leaders lost their lives because they did not understand the De-zombification process. They start a fight for the people they love dearly. At the end, the people turn against them. They have forgotten the lesson that they must first open the eyes of the people through education and then fight for them, not the other way around.

Zombie spectacle is particularly common in Africa and especially in Haiti. Zombification is a discipline that requires some occult knowledge not only about the human psyche but also certain plants and animal toxins. Zombification allows the Voodoo Priest to have total control over the psyche of an individual. In a sense, a zombie is a person who is being de-intellectualized.

The science of the human psyche has been around since the time of the gods. Our ancestors were highly advanced psychologists and scientists. They have utilized many techniques of the science of the psyche to help cure various psychosomatic illnesses. These secret techniques have been passed on from generation to generation. This advanced science of the psyche has not been written down. It follows that many people do not understand it. Of course, books on this subject are rare. Consequently, people do not have access to study it. Therefore, it remains hidden for centuries. It is believed to be dangerous knowledge (The Power of Knowledge, Chapter 1). Of course, controlling the human psyche could be dangerous if it is used maliciously.

However, this knowledge can also apply in various ways that can help humanity. The European Scientific Community and other government sectors are fascinated by this secret knowledge. They have experimented with monkeys, and they have understood some of the techniques. However, as time passes, most of the advanced techniques have been lost. The secret knowledge of the psyche has the potential to open the door to a whole new way to help those individuals who are mentally anguished.

However, many people around the world do not believe in the existence of zombies. They often associate a zombie story with fictitious, scary characters in movies. However, you would find both Africans and Haitians truly believe in zombie. Many may not understand the techniques involved. However, they are aware of the consequences. That is the reason why young Haitian and Africans are programmed by their parents to be very polite to everyone. They are aware of the fact that being impolite to an individual could destroy their lives. They do not want to be a victim of zombification for stupid reasons. Most Haitians have heard stories from friends and families. Believe it or not, many of the stories may sound like science fiction, but some of them are true.

Remember, zombification is used in Haiti as a deadly, secret form of retaliation against an aggressor. Therefore, you may find a few among the youths that still do not know about it. You should not be a surprise. Many people still do not know who were Martin Luther King Jr., Toussaint Louverture, Mahatma Gandhi and the like.

Some Voodoo Priests will not involve in zombification and will not kill for money. They mainly focus on healing their fellow humans for free or a small donation. However, many will kill for money, and will not turn down a large sum.

After the accuser had responded to several questions, the Voodoo Priest accepted to conduct a deadly attack against the suspect. Depending on the condition, the objective could be to make a zombie out of him. This form of justice is usually unfair, where the defendant has no chance to defend himself. If a Voodoo Priest falls in compassion with the accuser, the criminal zombie will endure some serious punishment, ordinarily in the form of beating and forced labor. Usually, the plaintiff is invited to come to assist and to participate in the beating.

Voodoo masters know how to make a powerful magic portion. It is a combination of bacterial toxins and other organic, chemical compounds. The mixture is turned into a powerful drug that can penetrate the skin of the victim. Upon contact with this drug, the victim becomes ill. After a couple of days, his vital signs such as his heartbeats and his breathing appear to stop. In fact, they are only slowed down so significantly that they cannot be detected without a highly sophisticated and advanced Electroencephalogram (EEG). The victim slowly enters a slow living condition called "a state of hibernation" or "catalepsy". The victim does not need much air to stay alive even underground for about a couple of days. During hibernation, if an electroencephalogram (EEG) is connected to the body of the victim, his brain waves activities will be detected. Because Haiti is an impoverished country, people of a small village do not make use of such expensive and sophisticated medical equipment. They use their fingers to look for vital signs. As a result, they mistakenly bury people, while their brains are still functioning. Hibernated victims are still aware of what is going on around them. They can hear their families and friend's voices, while they are completely paralyzed.

Victims are pronounced dead, and their families decided to bury them. The next day after the burial ceremony, the voodoo master and his crew go to the cemetery. They unbury their apparently dead bodies and bring them to a ceremonial place to be reconditioned. Then they put them in a plantation area to work as slaves. They accept to do whatever the voodoo priest instructs them to do.

Zombies are being fed a particular diet to keep them obedient for the rest of their lives. The voodoo master does not restrain his zombies. He does not have to; he sends them out on errands anywhere he likes. However, he has instructed them to avoid public gathering, families and friends attentions.

If a zombie manages to regain previous beta consciousness, he will be able to re-identify himself with his previous, personal, conditioned memories. Then, he will remember his families, and where he used to live. Although his ability to think remains weak, he still can explain certain things. The Voodoo Priest does not want something like that to happen. Therefore, if the zombie is caught with improved thinking abilities, he is being marked as "dangerous" (The Power of Knowledge, Chapter 1). If he did not manage to escape, and the Voodoo master cannot get him back to zombie consciousness, he will be killed immediately. The chance of this to happen is slim; however, it happens once in a while.

A zombie will not believe you if you walk up to him and say, "You are a zombie, slave of the Voodoo Priest; you must escape; come with me." He will rather run away or throw something at you. To help a zombie, you must know how to approach him. To avoid a violent reaction, you must know what to do and what to say. If the zombie is a strong man, you run the risk of getting hurt. When the Voodoo Master is getting too old and cannot take care of his zombies anymore, he just gives them in exchange. He transfers the load to another Voodoo Master. However, as mentioned above, many Voodoo Priests do not practice this atrocity. They are practicing natural healing for a small fee or donation.

There are many real stories about zombies encounter. Let me tell you a couple of them. Let's start with the story of Clairvius Narcisse. This story was all over the Internet. It happened in the year 1962, in Haiti.

Clairvius Narcisse entered Albert Schweitzer Hospital in the community of Deschapelles on April 30, 1962, and he was declared dead on May 3, 1962 by his doctor. Amazingly, eighteen years later Clairvius Narcisse was found wondering around in a marketplace, alive. What happened to him? Why did he not return home immediately?

After Clairvius Narciss had been buried, a Voodoo Master with his gang secretly went to the cemetery and unburied his body. They took him to a ceremonial place to be conditioned. Then, he was brought to a sugar plantation where he was instructed to work for the rest of his life.

After being conditioned, a zombie has no free will. His life's purpose is to execute the will and only the will of his master, the Voodoo Priest. Fortunately, a couple of years later, the Voodoo Priest died. As a result, Clairvius had no one to control his mental condition. Because he had been conditioned and lost his personal memories, he could not remember his address and who he was. Therefore, he could not return home. Clairvius spent many years wondering around in an amnesic, zombie state of mind. Partly under the voodoo priest's induced instructions, he unconsciously avoided anyone who might recognize him. Little by little his normal, personal memories started to return.

One day, while wondering around in a marketplace, probably in search of something to eat, he recognized his sister. He approached her and identified himself as Clairvius Narcisse.

At first glance, his sister could not identify him. Then, he told her secrets, family stories that nobody else would know except a family member. His sister was in shock, and she wanted to know where he has been all this time.

He explained that he was working as a zombie slave in a sugar cane field, and he managed to escape. To make the story short, they brought in the doctor who took care of him while he was hospitalized at Albert Schweitzer Hospital. Then they brought the priest who did his funeral ceremony when he was dead. Both positively recognized him as Clairvius Narcisse.

To be able to recognize and capable to approach his sister to identify himself as Clairvius Narcisse is an indication that he has partially been regained previous human consciousness. He was no longer operating under the Voodoo Priest's induced memory, which is a crucial component of the zombie's state of consciousness. Under the Voodoo

Priest induced memory, a zombie would rather hide or run away from his families and friends instead of approaching them.

Another amazingly true story of a zombie encounter happened in Plaisance, another small community in Haiti.

There was a catholic priest named "Père Codada"; the English translation is "Father Codada". He was from a small village located on the north side of Plaisance called Baron. He has been sent as the priest of the village of Plaisance. Père Codada was well known in the area. The people loved him as much as he loved them. He took the decision to organize a mandatory conversion of all Voodoo Priests in the community of Plaisance to Catholicism.

Because the people of the community loved him so much, most of them accepted to support this decision. He went over every Voodoo Master's home in the community and ceremonial places he could find, and he demanded to destroy all objects that are related to voodoo practices. Père Codada was so influential and powerful, not even one Voodoo Priest openly resisted his decision. In fact, he had almost everyone in the community behind him. Trying to resist him was an act of suicide. The people of the community will kill you if you refuse. Many Voodoo Priests voluntarily invited him to come to destroy all of their voodoo related stuff. One particular Voodoo Priest, Tipiké, reluctantly accepted Père Codada's proposition. He claimed to be ready for conversion. When Père Codada had entered Tipiké's ceremonial temple, there were many zombies. Tipiké accepted to liberate the zombies and gave them to Père Codada. Tipiké did not have a choice. After his conversion and the liberation of the zombies, Père Codada brought every zombie home back to his family. The people in the community were delighted. As a result, they viewed Père Codada as a God-sent.

One of the zombies is the sister of a woman called Madame Emogie, a good friend of my father. She used to live on Main Street, right across the Catholic Church. She has two daughters Paul and Lena. One of the girls, Paul, was a close friend of my father. She and my dad worked as professors at the "Ecole National des Garçons", translated as "National School for Boys". When my dad heard that Madame Emogie's sister, the dead one, had returned home. Out of curiosity, he decided to see for himself. My dad has a curious mind. He will not allow such event passes him by without notice. When my dad reached the house, there were so many people there the first couple of days. My father waited two more days. Then he went again; this time he saw the woman/zombie. She was alive; however, she seemed a little different than normal. She could talk, but she could not hold her head straight up. She had a small pillow placed between her head and her right shoulder. My father did not want to ask too many questions. His only question was,

"Why are you carrying a small pillow between your head and your shoulder?" She replied," While they were nailing my coffin a big nail stabbed my neck; therefore, I cannot hold my head straight up." In both accounts, the victims were no longer zombies. Why?

Because the victims have already regained previous consciousness, they are no longer zombies. Yes, they have been operated as zombies, but their minds have been liberated. They are partly free from both the effects of the drugs and the induced memory bank they used to identify themselves. The fact, that they could recognize their families and did not run away from them means that they were no longer zombies. Yes, they might have looked, talked, and acted a bit different from the normal average human. And, that was due to many long years of suffering, malnutrition, torture, and abuses. In addition to permanent, psychological damages caused by the un-relative quantity of administered drugs that caused the presumed "Cataleptic" stage, including various dosages of potent drugs to keep them in check from regaining previous consciousness. A real zombie is a person still under the influence of the Voodoo Master. He associates himself with what he can remember, which is only his new, induced memory. He is operating only under this new induced, fabricated, conditioned memory formed by the Voodoo Priest. You must remember this: To help a zombie, he must be removed from under the influence of the Voodoo Master.

When you're operating under the influence of the devil, you are similar to a zombie. You lack awareness of what is going on in the world. You exist to carry out the will of the devil. Your only savior in this predicament is awareness. And, it only comes with cognitive training, education, learning, diet, exercise, courage and persistence. Without awareness, again, you are like a zombie. The source of your mental entrapment will always remain hidden from your perception. Thus, taking the initiative to deal with your predicament without support is tough. The fact is: You do not seem to have any restraints to stop you from running away anymore. You go about your business with your hands and feet free of chuckles. You seem able to exercise your desire to do whatever you prefer. Therefore, you tend to reject the fact that you are a slave of the devil.

Rejection of the truth is the biggest mistake you could ever make. The Voodoo Priest does not confine his zombies. Because the zombie rejects the fact that he is a slave, he is unqualified to liberate himself. If he could remember who he was, he would immediately start to oppose and resist commands. The zombie accepts the situation as his new reality. If he happens to regain previous beta consciousness, his mind will bypass the induced memory, and he will no longer be a zombie. He may often disobey and react violently at times of commands. His real identity will start to show. He will remember his family, and where he used to live. He will be awake. Awake is not the right word. Let's say, he will be conscious of his predicament. He will immediately start to plan his escape to return home and to become the true him. If by a slight chance, he had been caught regaining the capability to think and reason, the Voodoo Priest would immediately recognize him as a "dangerous" man. If he cannot be brought back to his previous, zombie-like consciousness, he must be killed immediately, and that is, by any means. If not, he will be a threat to the Voodoo Priest's security and secrecies.

You may feel as if you are entering the esoteric realm of black magic. No, you are entering ***The Last Stratum,*** the realm of advanced knowledge of the science of the spirit of man. Apparently, this knowledge can be a bit scary, but keep calm. *You must prepare yourself to defend your planet and your people against all eventualities and evil.* **The Last Stratum** is your defense and your guidance. It will open your eyes and make you see the truth. It will show you how to detect and defend against various tricks of the devil.

The Last Stratum is not magic. It contains the teaching of your ancient ancestors who were the gods. It is rather your field of protection against the application of negative intelligence, the ultimate power of the devil. This system of knowledge has been in practice for eons. It serves as a powerful weapon for the Voodoo Master against his people. A small portion of this valuable knowledge is being exposed to you. Therefore, when the time is right, you will be able to recognize this malicious form of intelligence. The devil's negative intelligence against the human race is not something to overlook. You must be aware; for without awareness, continuous training and education, you do not stand a chance. The devil is already several steps ahead. You have to catch on.

It exists among us individuals that already regain original consciousness and cannot be brought back to ordinary human consciousness. We consider them as geniuses, freedom fighters, liberators, prophets and the like. On the other hand, due to the elite negative intelligent, he perceives them as "dangerous individuals". These people already take a stand to defend you against these malicious, elite societies. Therefore, they are already flagged, as "dangerous" human beings. The devil targets them to be ridiculed, denigrated, imprisoned or killed. We have to admit, the devil is exceptionally skilled. He is expert in the science of vilification of people's characters and negative propaganda. He is capable of manipulating your fragile mind and unconsciously inspire you to participate in his stupidities. He does not have to ask you for your permission. Using advanced techniques of negative intelligence, he successfully killed thousands of innocent Liberators and Prophets such as "Jesus Christ", Martin Luther King Jr.,

Malcolm X, Mahatma Gandhi, Toussaint Louverture, Thomas Sankara, and many others. Today, we have many men who already regained divine consciousness leaving among us. Our objective is to protect them from harms; therefore, it is important not to mention their names. One thing you must remember, the teaching of **The Last Stratum** is not intended to be political. Those parentheses have been opened just to stimulate flashes of awareness in a stagnant mind. The objective is to guide the student to a junction where he will have to question the truth and start to think for himself.

The fact is: The devil has already reconditioned you to accept a reduction of who you are as the reality of life. He has turned you into an inferior being and induced the feeling of inferiority through your mind. Your awareness is being reset into a zombie-like state. He is not only forcing you to think negatively of yourself, but he is also tricking you to accept his malicious, organized systems of greed such as exploitation, drugs, hatred, racism, defamation of character and organized crimes as your reality. We are back to what Mr. Joe X and Mr. John were trying to describe earlier. Negative Intelligence is the most devilish, selfish form of intelligence. You must prepare yourself to distinguish it. Although it is, as mentioned, a form of intelligence, it is contrary to what you usually consider as ordinary intelligence, which is the will of the gods. It looks and feels as if it is intelligence; however, it is not. It uses intelligence as its alias; therefore, it could easily pass for intelligence. You must prepare your mind to be able to make the distinction. It is used to control, abuse, and exploit the mentally exhausted, the poor and the masses. The practice of Negative Intelligence is responsible for 98% of human's sufferings on this planet. The ideology of *The Last Stratum* is preparing you to protect yourself. Your best chance is: Never stop learning and educating your mind. If you are ignorant of these facts, you are exceedingly weak, and you are at disadvantages. The devil is not only powerful, but he is also negatively intelligent. Therefore, choosing to remain ignorant already classified you as his slave without you even aware of that. You need to enter the realm of knowledge to qualify as a defender of your people. Otherwise, you do not stand a chance.

Continue reading; many interesting facts will be exposed in the next chapter.

But wait! You should not blame yourself if you feel that you have been traveled too fast and too deep into the field of advanced science of the human mind, keep calm. You must not forget that knowledge is power. It is the only thing without it, you will always be vulnerable.

~CHAPTER 11~

Extra

Relativity of God

Convolution of minds

"There will be a great battle tomorrow! "
"Who is fighting?"
"We are fighting!"
"We are?"
"Yes, we must fight to defend ourselves against aggressions of the White Army."
"Why is that? What's so great about the battle?"
"It is great because once and for all, our General will teach a lesson to the White Army. We are not something to mess with."
"Anyway!"

"The White Army has deployed his troops in area 24 along the border."

"Is this worth fighting for?"

"Of course, the White Army has no right to deploy his troop along the border on area 24. It is, perhaps, preparing for an invasion."

"INVASION…! You must be kidding!"

"After the last war, the land has been divided into half; each side has agreed to respect and sign the pact to keep the peace."

"Okay! But the White Army is in area 24. Its troops are closer to its territories than it is to ours. Where is the threat?"

"Well, area 24 is part of the border. No one has the right to violate the treaty of the war by deploying troops on any part of the border."

"Why is that?"

"It was written in the pact: *"Deploying your troops along any part of the border is an act of war."*

"ACT OF WAR! why?"

"The border has been reserved to wild lives, leisure and hunting, nothing else."

"Seriously, are you truly ready to give up your existence and die because of area 24?"

"Absolutely! I will fight to the death. Not for nothing but to defend the honor of my people and my territories."

"What people and what territories? We are miserable troops, always under the will of the General, and he is to decide when we should live or die."

"What's the big deal? Our General will fight for our benefits. He cares about us, and he refuses to let the white enemy steps down on us."

"Yes, but what about us? We are nothing. We keep fighting all the time, and I'm tired of this crap, okay! I have no hope to become general one day. Have you?"

"You have high ambitions, but, unfortunately, you ignore a great deal of the matter about what we are!"

"What is that? Fighting dogs?"

"No, far from that, we lack some intellectual capabilities. We are low level, virtual beings. We are the creation of the mind of our General."

"Oh no! You are degrading not only yourself but also every troop of our army who dies in battle every day. You are a disgrace!"

"No, our General has spent a great deal of his life studying battlefield strategies. He has been trained for that, and he spends every minute of his life thinking about the best

strategy to defend our honor against aggressions."

"Yes, But I do not like the idea that he is not physically involved in the battle. He has never been injured."

"Are you insane? Our General dedicated his mind and soul to the battle. He must stay alive to direct the action. Anyway, the battle is an invention of his mind. If he is dead, there is no battle; there is no us! We are doom!"

"I do not like his controlling of our lives. Especially, when he is to decide when we should die."

"I don't understand your dilemma. Your committing suicide to defend your territories is an honor. Such heroic action is the duty of every one of us."

"We should be able to see when it is necessary to commit suicide, not when our General decides to put an end to our lives."

"I do not get it! Why are you upset? Our General always calls for a suicide only when it is necessary. Again, it is always for our benefits. Anyway, you are still there; you are not dead yet."

"Yes, but I still do not like it."

"Let me tell you this, once and for all. We are not in the position to replace our General, Mr. Michel. It is impossible."

"IMPOSSIBLE! You must be kidding me! What are you implying?"

"We are imaginary beings. We only exist in the mind of our General. We are blips of electrical impulses."

"What do you mean?"

"What I meant is that. Our General is a super intelligent being with superior mental and intellectual properties."

"Are you implying that Mr. Michel, our General creates us?"

"You got that right. We exist only within the realm of the mind of our General. Outside of his mind, we are nothing. We do not exist."

"Because we are the product of the mind of our General, we can't conduct battles?"

"Absolutely. Imaginary beings do not exist outside of a mind. They coexist as a product of a mind. The battle and everything else is the creation of our General's mind."

"Is that means that I cannot have ambitions?"

"Well, you can. However, the desire to replace the mind that gave you existence can't be satisfied. Such ideology violates and goes against natural laws of the matrix of mind. And, that is assumed to be impossible."

"Wow! How did you know these? Who are you?"

"I am one of you. However, I obey, learn and study from the mind that gave me existence.

From this discipline, hopefully, one day, I will escape its imposed limitations."

"Yah!"

"This gives me the capability to see beyond actual perceptions of other imaginary beings in my category."

"Okay, we are imaginary, we exist only as an invention of the mind of our General, and we cannot replace the mind that gave us existence. What about our General?"

"I am glad you ask. Our General is also a product of another mind. He cannot replace or control the mind that gave him existence. Likewise, outside of that mind, he has no existence."

"Therefore, like me, many generals may not know that they are imaginaries."

"Yes, you hit the nail. Let's put it that way. A general is general in his realm. However, from

the perspective of the mind that gave him existence, he is imaginary."

"If I clearly understand, I'm only capable of controlling creations from my own mind. However, I cannot control the mind of our General?"

"Right-- but you can, only in some rare circumstances. However, our General, Mr. Michel, has to give you permission for that, do not count on it."

"Why?"

"This could be a high risk, possibly detrimental not only to us but also to the mind of our General. His mind gave us existence."

"So, this law also applies to our General?"

"Yes, this is a universal law. It applies to everyone. Generals can only control the imaginaries of their own minds. They can't control or replace the mind that gave them existence."

"Could our General manage to control the imaginaries of the mind of other generals?"

"**Yes, but extremely difficult. This is a closely guarded secret. If a general leaves the opportunity for outsiders to control his imaginaries, he is finished.**"

"Why?"

"**He risked losing every battle against his intruders. All generals keep their imaginaries carefully guarded against intruders and any forms of mental manipulations.**"

"How do generals manage to guard their imaginaries?"

"**As mentioned, it is a closely guarded secret, and we do not have time to discuss this occult subject now.**"

"In a sense, there is another mind that gave existence to the mind that gave existence to our General?"

"Of course, the mind system is made of layers upon layers. It is an infinite and complex system of minds that no one clearly understands."

"For instance, if we are imaginary beings, and the mind that gave us existence is our General's mind, how do you call the mind that gave existence to our General?"

"The mind that gave existence to our General is called God."

"From what you just told me, our General, Mr. Michel, is also an imaginary being?"

"Yes, only from the perspective of the mind that gave him existence. Like you, our General may not be aware of the fact that he is imaginary."

"Our General is imaginary? Amazing!"

"Yes, only from the perspective of the mind that gave him existence-- only."

"Therefore, everything is imaginary?"

"Yes, you can say that. In other terms, everything is operating in complex illusory dimensions of fields and frequencies."

"My head starts to spin. But, what kind of mind could possibly give existence to God?"

"Mr. Michel, our General, is knowledgeable about God; as I know about him. In fact, he is our God. Also, it is difficult to access mind systems beyond the layer of mind directly above yours."

"There must be some techniques to unlock the mysteries of these convoluted mind systems."

"Based on my researches, we are imaginary fields of mind of our General. On the other hand, our General is imaginary of the mind of God, and God his imaginary fields of the mind of Super God, and so on."

"Wow! Now that you open my eyes on the subject of minds, I would like to understand these mystical realms of levels of minds.

"Welcome to the universe of minds, and good luck!"

"This universe is complex beyond imagination, ah?"

"Yes, you can say that...Oops, it's already sunset. We must get ready for battle."

Conclusion:

Certainly, this book does not contain secrets of the earth and the sky, but it does contain occult and advanced knowledge of the human mind. However, the human mind is the ultimate apparatus that holds the secret of the earth and the sky. Oops!

Hopefully, you enjoy your journey with me through *The Last Stratum*, Volume I. And, you are looking forward to continuing this journey with me in the next volume.

Please, send your questions, critiques and recommendations to this email address: guirand@flaglex.com.

*Note: The above dialogue has been extracted from the book: **Initiation for General, Volume I**, by the same author. However, if you would like to know more about the convolution of minds as well as the relativity of God, you must read **The Last stratum, Volume II**.*

*Although the volumes of **The Last Stratum** could be read in any order, I, personally, recommend you not to read **The Last Stratum Volume II**, if you have not read **The Last Stratum, Volume I**.*

Index

aberration of superiority 65
accepted reality 87
adult's mind 44
advanced information 6, 7, 9, 10, 12
advanced knowledge 9
ancient ancestors 22, 25, 74, 88, 114
aspects of the reality 20
astrology 16, 17
avoid disclosure 94
become god 58, 90
Book of Thoth 16
brain circuitries 27, 29, 32, 45, 58
capability to think 113
cataleptic state 18
characteristics of a god 74
complex field 43
conscious observation 80
consciousness .. 8, 10, 13, 38, 58, 61, 62, 71, 74, 76, 82, 85, 86, 87, 88, 89, 91, 93, 102, 106, 110, 112, 115
criminalities 23

dangerous individuals	115
darkness of the mind	63
determination	76
development of writing	6
dimension of mind	90
dimensional images	37
dormant circuits	45, 47
dormant side	39
drugs	93, 110, 117
echolocation	47, 51, 52, 53, 57, 58
effects of rituals	49
electro encephalogram	101
esoteric realm	113
Excalibur	18
excellent manuscripts	15
exercise your desire	112
experienced	18, 83
Francois Duvalier	20
genuine awareness	22
godlike consciousness	74
Haiti	20, 94, 96, 99, 101, 104, 107
Hibernated victims	101
high priests	13

high-frequency pulses	51
Human Bat	54
human degradation	69
human development	17
human mind	10, 13, 24, 25, 28, 48, 57, 59, 60, 68, 78, 85, 89, 90, 93, 132
human psyche	9, 96, 97
human status	27, 28
human's memory	8
imaginaries	126, 127, 128
imagination	25, 46, 49, 59, 131
imposed limitations	25, 126
induced memory	95, 107, 111
induces visualization	86
information transfer	7
intelligence	16, 69, 72, 114, 117
Johannes Gutenberg	11
Karl Marx	21
knowledge is power	118
Lafayette Ron Hubbard	17
line of demarcation	61
linear spacetime	77
magical process	36

magical societies 7
malicious acts 31
Marxist ideologies 21
material vibrations 50
matter 23, 25, 26, 39, 42, 56, 84, 122
memory .8, 17, 73, 76, 78, 80, 82, 85, 86, 89, 91, 95, 106, 110, 112
mental balances 38, 43
mental interferences 89
mental power 19, 25, 90
millions of years 74
mind of the gods 65
natural law 40
natural laws of the matrix 125
negative intelligence 69, 114, 115
negative perception 60, 64
normal consciousness 8, 81, 85
normal operation 30
open mind 72, 88
ordinary consciousness 72
ordinary man 30, 42, 80, 88, 89, 91, 93
Perception 25
perfect accordance 85, 91

personal memories	91, 95, 105
physical symmetry	40
plasticity of the brain	33
powerful suggestions	55
previous consciousness	111
printing press	10, 11, 13
psychosomatic illnesses	97
Ramesses III	16
realm of transformation	62
relativity	20, 85, 133
Relativity of God	119
religious practices	11
second degree	19
Secret knowledge	98
somnambulism	22, 28
space and time	25, 78, 80
spacetime dissociation	78
spiritual techniques	8
suicide	16, 108, 123, 124
Super God	130
superior knowledge	7
supernatural powers	46
teachings of the gods	40

the Catholic Church........................... 10, 11, 109
the invention of writing 6
The Last Stratum 4, 20, 21, 22, 62, 86, 88, 90, 113, 114, 116, 117, 132, 133
the power to kill..17
the reader's psyche.................................. 15, 20
the truth 6, 23, 28, 48, 72, 86, 87, 90, 92, 96, 112, 114, 116
Thinking freely 86
Toussaint Louverture 23, 99, 116
true identity... 81, 112
true time..77
Universal Balance.................................... 41, 42
universal intelligence 26
universe of minds...131
using indulgences...11
voodoo masters..94
Voodoo Priests.......................99, 103, 107, 108
write in code..15
Young children...56
Zombification..................................... 94, 95, 96

Bibliography

Deeepak, Chopra. Ageless Body, Timeless Mind. Crown Publishing Group, 1994. ISBN 0517882124

Napoleon, hill. Keys to Success. Jeremy P. Tarcher/Penguin, 2008. ISBN 158542689X.

Karlins, Marvin and Andrews, Lewis. Biofeedback: Turning on the Power of Your Mind. Grand Central Pub, 1974. ISBN 9780446922005.

Isaac, Asimov. The Relativity of Wrong. Kensington Publishing Corporation, 1980. ISBN 155817169X.

L. Ron, Hubbard. Dianetics. Bridge Publications, Inc., 2007. ISBN 1403144842.

JohnRobertPosey. The Cordoba Bull Ranch Experiment. French Documentary. <http://www.youtube.com/watch?v=QwPUVqeWEos>.

BibliOdyssey. Galvanizing Aldini. February 03, 2007. <http://bibliodyssey.blogspot.com/2007/02/galvanizing-aldini.html>.

Special zombie Clervius: Junior Mengual Owner Ayiti Tan Lontan Part1, 2. *<https://www.youtube.com/watch?v=8iHXwoLRMA>.*

www.ingramcontent.com/pod-product-compliance
Lightning Source LLC
LaVergne TN
LVHW041628070426
835507LV00008B/501